Original title:

Spring's Blossoming Bliss

Author: Tim Wood

ISBN HARDBACK: 978-9916-85-774-8

ISBN PAPERBACK: 978-9916-85-775-5

Whispered Dewdrops

As morning breaks, the dewdrops glisten,
Whispering tales that trees might listen.
Softly they land on petals bright,
Crystals of dawn, catching light.

In silence they dance on blades of grass,
Moments fleeting, like dreams that pass.
Each droplet carries the night's embrace,
A fleeting shimmer, a subtle grace.

A Kaleidoscope of Growth

In every seed a story waits,
The whispers of nature unlock the gates.
Colors collide in a vibrant play,
Creating a canvas that brightens the day.

From roots that dig deep in the earth's embrace,
To branches that stretch in a graceful chase.
A dance of life, a marvelous sight,
A symphony of growth, pure and bright.

Lush Landscapes Await

Beyond the hills where shadows hide,
Lush landscapes call, with arms spread wide.
Beneath the sky, so endless and blue,
A world unfolds, both wondrous and new.

Mountains rise with ancient grace,
Each valley holds a secret place.
Nature's palette in hues so grand,
Invites the heart to understand.

Dreaming in Color

Close your eyes and drift away,
Into a world where colors play.
Brushstrokes of joy in every hue,
A canvas of dreams, waiting for you.

Violet whispers and emerald sighs,
Crimson laughter beneath the skies.
In this realm where wishes soar,
Every heartbeat opens a door.

Playful Breezes

Whispers of the wind dance through the trees,
Caressing leaves with gentle ease.
Laughter twirls on soft golden light,
As day gives way to sweet twilight.

They tease the flowers, bright and bold,
In hues that shimmer, tales unfold.
Each gust a story, each sigh a song,
In nature's chorus, we all belong.

Nature's Embrace

In the forest's arms, I find my peace,
Tender moss and sunlight, a soft release.
Rippling streams weave a soothing tune,
As shadows dance beneath the moon.

Birds serenade with melodies sweet,
While blossoms sway in rhythmic beat.
Every breeze carries a promise anew,
In nature's embrace, I am me, I am you.

The Return of Color

Winter's retreat, a canvas so grey,
Spring nudges softly, brushing skies to play.
Emerald greens sprinkle the hills,
With saffron blooms that chase the chills.

Golden sunsets splash warmth afar,
And silvery stars ignite the star.
With every bloom and every hue,
The world awakens, refreshed and true.

Resilient Roots

Amidst the storms that rage and roar,
A testament of strength, we explore.
Deep in the ground, where shadows loom,
Roots intertwine, dispelling gloom.

With every crack, they push and grow,
Harnessing the strength of the earth below.
Resilience whispers in whispers loud,
From humble beginnings, we stand proud.

Awakening Petals

In the hush of dawn's embrace,
The flower's heart begins to wake,
Softly stretching towards the sky,
Awakening petals, a vibrant ache.

Beneath the dew, a secret stirs,
Colors burst with gentle grace,
Nature's breath, a sweet reminder,
Life's renewal in every place.

Sunlight trickles through the leaves,
And whispers stories of old dreams,
Each petal tells of hopeful mornings,
Where beauty reigns and laughter gleams.

Serenade of New Beginnings

A tender breeze begins to play,
Caressing blooms in warm sunlight,
It sings a song of fresh tomorrows,
Where shadows fade and dreams take flight.

With every bud, a story forms,
Of journeys waiting to unfold,
An orchestra of colors bright,
In gardens kissed by spring's soft hold.

The world awakens, filled with glee,
As nature whispers in sweet refrain,
A serenade of new beginnings,
In harmony, our hearts remain.

The Dance of Daffodils

Golden trumpets sway and twirl,
In meadows bright, they set the stage,
Their vibrant heads nod in delight,
As springtime's spirit turns the page.

Each petal sways to nature's tune,
A graceful waltz beneath the sun,
With every gust, they bend and bow,
In joyful dance, they're never done.

They whisper stories of the morn,
Of sunlight kissed by gentle rain,
In daffodil's embrace, we learn,
That life's a dance, with joy as gain.

Whispers of Fresh Green

In the forest's heart, where silence lays,
A carpet of green, soft and bright,
Whispers of freshness fill the air,
In every leaf, a promise of light.

The trees stand tall with arms outspread,
Embracing each chance for growth anew,
A symphony of life unfurls,
In shades of emerald, rich and true.

The world awakens from its slumber,
Each blade of grass, a joyful prayer,
Whispers of fresh green sing to us,
Inviting hearts to breathe and share.

Nature's Color Palette

In the whispering woods where the wildflowers
sway,
A canvas of colors unfolds day by day,
Emerald greens dance with golden beams,
While azure skies cradle soft, drifting dreams.

The sunset spills hues of crimson and gold,
As the tales of the evening begin to be told,
Nature's brush strokes, both fierce and tender,
In each vibrant hue, a reminder to remember.

Cascading Cherry Blossoms

In spring's gentle embrace, the cherry trees
bloom,
A flurry of petals dispelling all gloom,
Soft whispers of pink in the breeze gently float,
As nature's sweet symphony begins to remote.

The ground wears a carpet of delicate lace,
With laughter and love, we gather in grace,
Each blossom a promise, each petal a sigh,
A moment of beauty that never says goodbye.

The Awakening Grove

In the hush of the dawn where the wild things
roam,
The grove stirs awake, finding solace at home,
With rustling leaves that lowly hum songs,
And sunlight that dances, where each creature
belongs.

The ancient trees stand, guardians of time,
Whispering secrets in nature's sweet rhyme,
As flowers unfurl in a tender embrace,
Life's vibrant renewal, a sacred space.

Vibrant Echoes of Dawn

When the morning light spills over mountains so
proud,
Whispers of dawn wake the earth from its shroud,

With birdsong and laughter that bubbles like
streams,
A new day unfolds, igniting our dreams.

Golden rays spill warmth on the dewy green
grass,
Beckoning shadows, as night fades to pass,
In this vibrant chorus, the world seems to glow,
Painting the moments for all souls to know.

Colorful Embrace

In gardens where the sunlit flowers dance,
Their colors weave a bright, enchanting trance,
With every petal, stories softly sing,
A tapestry of life, on breezes cling.

Reds and yellows blend in joyful surprise,
While blues and greens lift hearts to the skies,
Together, they create a vivid frame,
An ever-changing canvas without shame.

The Rise of Petals

From sleeping buds in shadows held so tight,
Emerging gently toward the morning light,
Each petal opens wide, embracing day,
A symphony of colors on display.

With fragile grace, they rise, a bold parade,
Against the crispness of the cool, soft shade,
Their beauty speaks of worlds both fresh and
new,
A promise wrapped in nature's tender hue.

Awakening Vibrance

As dawn unfolds her arms to greet the morn,
The sleepy fields of greenness feel reborn,
Vibrancy erupts in hues both bright and bold,
Nature's palette weaving stories yet untold.

With every breeze, the petals start to sway,
A dance of life that beckons through the day,
Awakening the heart to blissful grace,
In every blossom, find a warm embrace.

Blossoms Against the Sky

Against the azure stretch, the blossoms glow,
Their colors burst like laughter in the flow,
Petals reach out, they flirt with clouds so high,
In whispered dreams, they kiss the endless sky.

With every drop of rain, they swell with cheer,
A canvas bright that draws us ever near,
Each flower stands, a radiant declaration,
In their sweet fragrance lies our jubilation.

The Herald of Warmth

In the dawn's gentle grasp, sunlight appears,
Whispering warmth to the frozen ground,
Herald of spring, banishing fears,
With every ray, new joys are found.

Blossoms unfurl in vibrant hues,
Dancing lightly on the softening breeze,
Nature awakens, as if to choose,
Life's sweet promise in rustling trees.

Awakening in Petal Rain

Delicate drops fall from skies so clear,
Petals cascade like whispers untold,
In each gentle kiss, the world draws near,
A symphony of colors, vibrant and bold.

The fragrance of blossoms fills the air,
As nature rejoices in this tender embrace,
Awakening spirits, banishing despair,
In each petal rain, we find our place.

Awakening Petals

Amidst the slumber, petals unfold,
Awakening dreams in the morning light,
Colors emerge from the threads of gold,
Nature's artistry, a wondrous sight.

With every sunrise, new stories arise,
Echoing softly through the fields so wide,
Awakening petals beneath azure skies,
Unveiling the beauty that blossoms inside.

Fresh Breeze Whispers

A fresh breeze whispers secrets untold,
Through the branches where shadows dance,
Carrying tales of the brave and the bold,
In the rustling leaves, an enchanting trance.

It stirs the heart with a gentle embrace,
Bringing warmth from the sun's golden hue,
In the melody of nature's grace,
Every whisper feels like a love that is true.

Garden of Awakening

In the hush of dawn's soft embrace,
Flowers unfurl with a gentle grace,
Petals glisten, kissed by dew,
Nature awakens, fresh and new.

Whispers of life in fragrant air,
Butterflies dance without a care,
Sunbeams paint the earth in gold,
Stories of beauty, waiting to be told.

Whispering Meadows

Gentle winds caress the ground,
In whispering meadows, peace is found,
A symphony of rustling leaves,
Nature speaks, and the heart believes.

Grasses sway like thoughts unkept,
In the quiet, dreams are swept,
Each blade a verse of silent cheer,
In the meadows, all is clear.

The Laughter of Blossoms

Bright blooms burst forth in joyful laughter,
Colors colliding, a vibrant chapter,
Beneath the sun, their joy cascades,
As if to sing of sunlight's parades.

Each petal giggles in the breeze,
An echo of life, a moment to seize,
In this laughter, troubles fade,
A tapestry of joy is laid.

Renewal's Palette

Brushstrokes of spring paint the air,
Every hue a promise laid bare,
From winter's grasp, life breaks free,
A canvas of renewal, for all to see.

The whisper of earth, a call to revive,
In nature's embrace, the spirit will thrive,
With each bloom, hope is redefined,
In renewal's palette, joy we find.

Harmony in Bloom

In whispers soft, the petals speak,
Colors dance in rhythm, unique.
A symphony of nature's grace,
Where hearts unite in this sacred space.

Beneath the sun, the flowers sway,
In fragrant bursts, they greet the day.
With every bud, a story told,
In harmony, life's beauty unfolds.

The Charm of Emerging Leaves

As spring unfolds, the leaves appear,
Emerald whispers, vibrant and clear.
They stretch their limbs to greet the skies,
Embracing warmth as the cold subsides.

In dappled light, there's magic found,
Nature's canvas, lush and profound.
With every breath, they sway and dance,
A fleeting moment, a fleeting chance.

Awakened Beauty

A gentle hush, the dawn's embrace,
Awakening beauty, a sacred space.
Butterflies flutter, in delicate flight,
Kissing the blooms, in morning light.

The dewy petals, soft and bright,
Whisper secrets of the night.
In every corner, life renews,
Awakened beauty, the world imbues.

Garden Echoes

In gardens lush, where shadows play,
Echoes of laughter drift away.
Every flower tells a tale,
Of sunshine bright and gentle hail.

The rustle speaks, the breezes sigh,
Footfalls of dreams that wander by.
In every path, a memory glows,
In whispered thoughts, the garden knows.

Radiant Awakening

In the golden glow of dawn's embrace,
Night's shadow fades, in daylight's grace.
Whispers of hope dance on the breeze,
As the world awakens, hearts find their ease.

Sunbeams spill like laughter on the ground,
Nature's canvas, rich and profound.
Every petal and leaf, a story unfolds,
A symphony of colors, vibrant and bold.

The sky blushes softly with hues of rose,
As slumbering dreams in the light decompose.
Each moment bursting with life anew,
In radiant awakenings, we find our view.

Butterflies and Blossoms

Among the blooms where laughter sings,
Butterflies flutter on delicate wings.
Nature's palette in hues so bright,
A dance of delight in the morning light.

Petals unfurl, a fragrant delight,
As soft winds carry dreams into flight.
In gardens where colors effortlessly blend,
Life whispers secrets that never end.

Each butterfly a painter, the world its art,
Creating beauty that captivates the heart.
For in this moment, as joys entwine,
The magic of life feels both grand and divine.

The Symphony of Growth

In silent realms where roots spread wide,
Life's symphony plays, a mythic tide.
Seeds of tomorrow, sown in the ground,
Echoing dreams where hope can be found.

With every raindrop a note that inspires,
The gentle rain fuels the heart's fires.
From tender sprouts to the tallest trees,
Growth is a melody carried by the breeze.

Seasons will change, yet harmony's near,
In every hardship, our strength appears.
Through challenges faced, we rise and sing,
The symphony of growth is a glorious thing.

Meadow's Gentle Embrace

In meadows wide where the wildflowers sway,
The dance of the grasses invites us to play.
Sun-kissed and free, beneath the vast skies,
Nature's soft whispers are sweet lullabies.

The air is adorned with scents rich and warm,
A haven of peace, a tranquil charm.
Here, in the stillness, we find our release,
In meadow's embrace, our burdens decrease.

Clouds drift lazily, a canvas above,
Each moment captured, a gift wrapped in love.
As time gently waltzes, let worries all cease,
In the meadow's soft hold, we discover our peace.

Dappled Sunshine and Fresh Earth

In the cradle of a whispering grove,
Where shadows dance in golden beams,
Sunlight dapples the fresh, sweet earth,
Nurturing dreams in sun-kissed streams.

Leaves twinkle with stories untold,
As breezes weave through branches wide,
Each ray, a promise of warmth and gold,
In nature's heart, where hopes abide.

The Embrace of Soft Rain

A gentle touch from heaven above,
The world awash in silver grey,
Soft rain descends like a mother's love,
Each droplet whispers, 'Stay, oh stay.'

Pavements shimmer, reflections gleam,
Leaves awaken with a verdant sigh,
In the quiet, nature's dream,
Embraced by rain beneath the sky.

Colorful Echoes of Dawn

As night surrenders to the light,
A canvas brushed with hues anew,
Colorful echoes take to flight,
Painting the sky with every hue.

Birds sing songs of joy and cheer,
While the sun spills warmth on waking lands,
In each corner, magic draws near,
Dawn's gentle touch, with open hands.

Butterflies in Bloom

In gardens where the flowers sway,
Butterflies flit on gossamer wings,
Each blossom beckons them to play,
A ballet of nature, as spring sings.

Colors burst from petals bright,
A tapestry of life unfurled,
While butterflies dance, a fleeting sight,
Celebrating the beauty of the world.

A Tapestry of Renewal

In the cradle of dawn, where shadows recede,
Colors awaken, fulfilling the need.
Threads of the past weave through present's
design,
A tapestry bright, as the sun starts to shine.

Each leaf whispers stories of seasons gone by,
In the dance of the branches, the spirits fly high.
With every new bloom, the promise returns,
In the heart of the earth, the fire of life burns.

The Heart of Nature

In quiet meadows, where wildflowers bloom,
The heartbeat of nature dispels all gloom.
Streams sing a melody, soft and sincere,
Whispers of life, echoing near.

Winds weave their secrets through arms of the trees,
While mountains look on, resolute as the seas.
Nature's embrace is a balm, a delight,
In her verdant expanse, all wrongs find their right.

Colorful Resurgence

A palette of colors unfurls in the light,
As spring sheds her cloak, bringing warmth to the
night.
With every petal that softly unfurls,
The promise of joy, as the world twirls and swirls.

Golden sunbeams dance on dew-kissed green,
Awakening whispers of magic unseen.
Through canopies lush, where shadows do play,
Life's vibrant cycle begins a new day.

The Renewal of Life

In the hush of the forest, where soft shadows
creep,
The cycle of life stirs from a deep sleep.
With every heartbeat, a promise is cast,
Renewal ignites, as we honor the past.

With gentle caresses, the rain starts to fall,
Nurturing seeds that lay dormant, though small.
From struggle to bloom, resilience will thrive,
In the tapestry woven, we find we're alive.

The Splendor of Now

In the stillness of the moment, time pauses to
breathe,
A vibrant tapestry unfolds, where dreams weave,
Each heartbeat a reminder, a silent vow,
To cherish every breath, in the splendor of now.

Golden rays of sunlight dance upon the dew,
Whispers of the universe echo, soft and true,
Captured in the heartbeat, eternity takes a bow,
Inviting our souls to dwell in the splendor of now.

Whispers of the Meadow

In the meadow where the wildflowers play,
Nature sings a melody, gentle and sway,
Each petal a note in a symphonic blend,
Whispers of the earth, where all sorrows mend.

Bees hum a rhythm, butterflies flit by,
Beneath a vast canvas of azure sky,
The breeze carries stories of love and of light,
In this sacred embrace, everything feels right.

Harmony in the Air

As the wind caresses leaves with a tender sigh,
A symphony of life plays, soaring high,
Birds trill a chorus, a sweet serenade,
Harmony in the air, where worries fade.

Clouds, like cotton candy, drift lazily above,
Painting a picture of peace and of love,
Each moment's an echo of joy we can share,
Lost in the rhythm, the world becomes rare.

Bountiful Beginnings

In the cradle of dawn, where the day finds its
spark,
Each sunrise a promise, each shadow, a mark,
Seeds of hope are sown in the fertile ground,
Bountiful beginnings, where blessings abound.

With every heartbeat, a chance to renew,
Embracing the unknown, with courage to pursue,

Life unfolds like petals, vibrant and bright,
In the dance of beginnings, we find our true light.

The Canvas of Colors

On a vast expanse where the skies collide,
Brushstrokes of nature, side by side.
Crimson and gold in a dance so bright,
The canvas of colors, a pure delight.

Emerald whispers beneath the sun,
Each hue a story, together as one.
From violet dusk to the azure realm,
In the palette of life, our dreams overwhelm.

Melody of the Opening Bloom

In the hush of dawn, a symphony starts,
Petals unfurl, like music from hearts.
A soft serenade in the morning air,
Nature's sweet rhythm, beyond compare.

Every blossom croons in the gentle breeze,
Harmonies woven through rustling leaves.
As colors entwine in the sunlight's glow,
The melody sings of the beauty we know.

New Life in the Breeze

A whispering wind through the tall green grass,
Brings tales of rebirth as the seasons pass.
Tiny sprouts breaking through the earth's
embrace,
New life awakens with delicate grace.

With each breath of spring, hope is reborn,
In the cradle of warmth, a new day is sworn.
The breeze carries laughter, the joy of the free,
An orchestra playing in harmony with the trees.

Renewal's Sweet Embrace

When winter departs, leaving shadows behind,
Spring's tender fingers, in warmth intertwined.
A cradle of life where the dormant once slept,
In renewal's sweet embrace, the earth gently
wept.

The blooms brush the canvas of skies so blue,
With echoes of laughter, and whispers of dew.
Each moment, a promise of all that can be,
In the dance of the seasons, we find our key.

Laughter in the Meadow

In the meadow where wildflowers play,
Children's laughter dances in the sun's ray,
Butterflies flit on a whisper of breeze,
Joyful echoes ripple through the tall trees.

Barefoot adventures on soft emerald grass,
Tickling daisies as warm moments pass,
Giggles blend sweetly with nature's refrain,
A symphony of bliss, a melodic gain.

Sunlight glistens on water's embrace,
Every heart gathers in this sacred space,
With every burst of laughter we find,
The meadow may hold a peace so kind.

Here in the midst of nature's sweet charm,
Where laughter encircles like a gentle arm,
In each playful moment, we come alive,
A meadow of joy where our spirits thrive.

Sun-kissed Buds

Awakening gently beneath the first light,
Sun-kissed buds stretch, bathed in golden sight,
Nature whispers softly, promising new,
The dance of the blossoms begins with the dew.

Petals unfurl, in hues bright and bold,
Stories of spring in each petal unfold,
Crimson, and lavender, with scents that enchant,
A garden of dreams where the heart learns to
chant.

The breeze carries secrets through greenery's
arms,
Each sunlit moment holds nature's charms,
As life pushes forward in a glorious show,
In a world of sunflowers, we learn to grow.

With every heartbeat, the earth comes alive,
In sun-kissed buds, we remember to thrive,
Together we bloom, with love that expands,
Hand in hand with nature, we make our own
plans.

A Tapestry of Renewal

Weaving dreams as the seasons unfold,
Threads of the past, both vibrant and bold,
Each moment a stitch in life's intricate seam,
A tapestry painted with joy and with dream.

In the depths of the winter, we sow seeds of light,

Tendrils of hope reach out, taking their flight,
Through shadows of doubt where the cold winds
roam,
We nurture resilience, with warmth we call home.

The springtime brings whispers of promise so
bright,
New colors emerge, casting shadows of night,
Each flower a promise, each leaf a sweet rhyme,
In nature's embrace, we savor the time.

We gather our stories to craft a great whole,
A tapestry woven with heart and with soul,
With threads of togetherness, courage, and cheer,

In the fabric of life, we hold what is dear.

Joy in Bloom

Amidst the chaos, life spreads its wings,
Petals unfurl, as the heart softly sings,
In every color, a heartbeat displayed,
A garden of laughter where love won't fade.

Joy finds a place in the rise of the day,
Each bloom a reminder, in petals we play,
With the sun as a companion, we dance in the
light,
Chasing our shadows, alive in the sight.

The air is alive with sweet fragrant glee,
As wishes take flight, like the birds in the tree,
In every blossom, a story will thrive,
A testament to all that we feel so alive.

So gather the moments, let laughter consume,
Within every heartbeat, there's joy in full bloom,
Together we flourish, like fields rich and wide,
Forever united, in this beautiful ride.

The Hopeful Horizon

As dawn unfolds with colors bright,
The promise of a fresh new day,
Each golden ray ignites the night,
And banishes the dark away.

The sky, a canvas painted wide,
With dreams that dance on morning's breath,
In hope we stand, with faith as guide,
Embracing life, defying death.

With every step, our hearts do swell,
For futures rich with joy and grace,
In every tale that time will tell,
We seek the sun, we seek our place.

So lift your eyes to what's ahead,
The horizon calls, a beacon bright,
With every dawn, let go of dread,
And walk with love into the light.

Nature's Glorious Reawakening

In winter's grasp, the silence deep,
A slumber held in crystal snow,
But whispers call from earth's soft keep,
Awakening life, a vibrant glow.

The crocus blooms, a herald bold,
With violets peeking through the frost,
A tapestry of green and gold,
Nature's love, no longer lost.

The songbirds chirp, a rhythmic choir,
From branches bare, new nests are spun,
As seasons turn, our hearts aspire,
To dance with joy beneath the sun.

And rivers flow with laughter pure,
While blossoms sway in gentle breeze,
In nature's arms, we find the cure,
For all the world's unease.

Flourish in the Light

Beneath the sun, let spirits rise,
Unfurl like petals, bright and fair,
In every glance, a joy that lies,
A tender warmth in open air.

With laughter ringing through the trees,
Our dreams take flight on zephyr's wings,
The artist's brush doth paint with ease,
The beauty in what nature brings.

So bloom with purpose, fierce and bold,
Embrace the light, let shadows flee,
In every heart, a flame of gold,
A symphony of reverie.

So flourish, dear, and do not fear,
The light within will guide your way,
With open arms, draw near, draw near,
To joyous dawns, to bright new days.

Gardens of New Beginnings

In secret spaces, hope takes root,
Where whispered dreams in silence grow,
From tiny seeds to branches stout,
A testament to life's sweet flow.

Each petal holds a tale untold,
Of rain and sun, of joy and tears,
In vibrant hues, the brave and bold,
Stand witness to their hopes and fears.

From barren soil to lush delight,
The gardens weave their magic spell,
With every bloom, the heart takes flight,
In fragrant echoes, deep we dwell.

So sow with love, and nurture time,
For from the earth, new dreams shall spring,
In gardens wide, our hearts will chime,
A choir sweet, in life's offering.

Dreams of Green

In the quiet of the dawn, the emerald dreams
arise,
Whispers of the earth caress the waking skies.
Blades of grass dance softly, a vibrant serenade,
As dewdrops glisten brightly, nature's jewels
displayed.

Through meadows wide and valleys deep, the
colors softly blend,
A tapestry of life unfolds, where every trail may
bend.
The song of gentle breezes, a lullaby to hear,
In dreams of green, we find our peace, our spirits
linger near.

Radiance Beneath the Frost

Beneath the icy surface, a glow begins to beat,
In slumber lies the magic, where warmth and chill
shall meet.
Crystal shards fall gently, like whispers through
the night,
Yet life is brewing quietly beneath the silver light.

With each reluctant sunrise, the thaw begins to
sing,
A promise of the flowers, the joy that spring can
bring.
Though frost may hide the beauty, and shadows
stretch their sway,
The radiance beneath the frost will soon reclaim
the day.

Nature's Gentle Rebirth

Awake, the world is stretching, as winter bids
goodbye,
A tapestry of colors and fragrances draw nigh.
The crocus breaks the silence, a harbinger of
light,
As nature's gentle rebirth ignites the day from
night.

With every bloom and blossom, the earth's own
lullaby,
A symphony of petals from the ground to reach
the sky.
The woodlands hum with life anew, as creatures
come to play,
In nature's gentle rebirth, we find our hearts
convey.

Petals Unfurling

Petals unfurling slowly, like secrets laid to rest,
Each color tells a story, in nature's tender vest.
From whispers soft to blushing hues, like lovers
in a trance,
The garden blooms with laughter, inviting souls
to dance.

Amidst the sun-kissed blossoms, the world begins
to spin,
The fragrance drifts on breezes, a sweet and
vibrant hymn.
Each petal holds a promise, of what the heart may
feel,
In nature's grand display, our dreams become the
real.

Gentle Sunbeams

Gentle sunbeams kiss the earth,
Awakening life, a moment of mirth.
Whispers of warmth in the cool morning air,
Nature unfolds, her beauty laid bare.

Dancing shadows in the golden light,
Each blade of grass, a jewel bright.
In this soft glow, the world seems to pause,
A symphony of silence, nature's applause.

The flowers stretch out, reaching for sky,
As clouds drift lazily, letting time fly.
With every dawn, a promise renews,
In gentle sunbeams, hope is infused.

So let us revel in this tranquil scene,
In the heart of nature, forever serene.
For each sunbeam is a story to tell,
A reminder that all can fare well.

Nature's Reclamation

In shadows where silence dared to creep,
Nature awakens from her deep sleep.
With emerald tendrils, she breaks through the
stone,
An echo of life in a once-lost throne.

Vines entwine ruins, a tender embrace,
While wildflowers bloom with a delicate grace.
The whispers of trees tell tales from the past,
Of a world where the wild and the free hold fast.

Through cracked pavements, she finds her way,
Transforming the remnants of yesterday.
As cities grow quiet, she sings her sweet song,
Nature's reclamation, fierce and strong.

Each rustling leaf, a vibrant refrain,
A testament to life, enduring through pain.
Let us remember, as we walk our own path,
Nature's resilience, her unyielding wrath.

Petals of Promise

In gardens where colors collide and dance,
Petals unfurl in a fragile romance.
Each hue whispers secrets, both old and new,
A tapestry woven with morning dew.

The daffodils nod, while the roses stand tall,
Each blossom a story, a fragile call.
Through seasons of sorrow, through laughter and
tears,
Petals of promise dispel all our fears.

Butterflies flutter, painting the air,
Awakening dreams that once seemed rare.
Amidst the blossoms, a hopeful refrain,
A reminder that beauty can bloom after pain.

With every small bud that dares to arise,
We find strength in fragility, beauty in ties.
For in every petal lies life's gentle grace,
A promise that love will forever embrace.

A Canvas of Life

Underneath vast skies where colors entwine,
Nature's brush paints a canvas divine.
With strokes of fierce sunsets, soft dawns in hues,

We're reminded that life is an endless muse.

Mountains rise boldly, standing their ground,
While rivers weave stories, with whispers
profound.
Every breeze carries tales from afar,
A gallery of moments, beneath every star.

In fields of wildflowers, laughter and play,
Children run freely, in the warmth of the day.
Each moment we cherish, a stroke in our heart,
Creating a masterpiece, each life a fine art.

So let us embrace this vibrant design,
For we are the colors that perfectly shine.
United in wonder, with nature as our guide,
We paint our existence, with love as our stride.

The Dance of the Daffodils

In gentle breezes, they sway and spin,
Golden trumpets shout the joy within,
Petals glistening like morning dew,
A dance of spring, where dreams come true.

Their laughter echoes through fields so bright,
As sunlight drapes the earth in golden light,
With every whisper, they turn and twirl,
A waltz of nature, the daffodils' swirl.

Nature's Joyful Rebirth

From winter's slumber, the earth awakes,
A symphony played by the softest flake,
Green shoots arise from the warm, rich ground,
Life's tender melodies in every sound.

The blossoms burst with a fragrant cheer,
Each petal a promise that spring is near,
Nature's palette paints with vibrant hue,
In every corner, hope is born anew.

Colors of the Heart

In shades of crimson, love's fire burns,
While sapphire waves in the ocean churns,
Emerald leaves whisper secrets untold,
A canvas of feelings, both vivid and bold.

Golden laughter dances on the breeze,
In lilac dreams where the spirit finds ease,
Each color a harmony, a story to part,
The vivid reflections of the human heart.

Chrysanthemum Dreams

In twilight gardens, the blooms unfold,
Chrysanthemums whispering secrets of old,
Their petals like lanterns in soft, dusky light,
Illuminating hopes in the hush of the night.

With every breath, a promise of peace,
A silent prayer for love's sweet release,
In vibrant clusters, they gather and sway,
Chrysanthemum dreams guiding the way.

Garden of Whispers

In the quiet glade where secrets dwell,
Gentle breezes weave a tender spell,
Petals quiver, whisper soft and sweet,
As sunlight dances on the mossy seat.

Every leaf a story, every root a song,
Nature's pulse throbs where hearts belong,
In shadows deep, where wildflowers bloom,
The garden calls us to its fragrant room.

Here the murmurs of the earth resound,
In hidden corners, love can be profound,
With every rustle, old tales revive,
In the garden of whispers, we come alive.

Blossoms Beneath the Sun

Golden rays spill upon the verdant ground,
Petals stretch wide, a beauty unbound,
In the light of day, the colors ignite,
A symphony rich, a joyous delight.

Dancing in breezes that carry their song,
Blossoms sway gently, where dreams belong,
Cloaked in a warmth that the sun bestows,
Each moment a treasure, where pure beauty
grows.

They whisper of summer, of life in full bloom,
In gardens aglow, no hint of gloom,
Beneath the sun's gaze, they thrive and they play,

A canvas of colors kissed by the day.

Verdant Dreams Unfurled

In the heart of the forest, where shadows retreat,
Lies a carpet of green, where earth and sky meet,
Moss-covered stones cradle secrets of old,
While whispered ambitions in leaves unfold.

Cascading streams sing a melody clear,
Flowing with visions that nature holds dear,
A tapestry woven with threads of pure grace,
In the verdant embrace, we find our place.

Awakening dreams in the cool morning light,
With every new dawn, the world feels so bright,
Nature unveils its enchanting appeal,
In verdant dreams unfurled, our spirits heal.

Nature's Love Letter

On the edge of a hill where wildflowers grow,
Nature pens letters in the soft breeze's flow,
Each petal a promise, each breeze a caress,
In the arms of the earth, we find tenderness.

Rivers write verses on stones worn and sleek,
Their laughter a language that lovers can speak,
With whispers of longing, the trees sway in tune,
As night wraps us gentle 'neath the watchful
moon.

Stars twinkle like jewels, a magnificent sight,
In this love letter crafted by day and by night,
Nature's embrace is a heartfelt refrain,
A symphony rich, echoing love's sweet domain.

Life's Effervescent Palette

Brushstrokes of laughter, hues of delight,
Dancing through shadows, embracing the light.
Every moment a splash, a vibrant refrain,
In the canvas of time, joy mingles with pain.

Whispers of dreams in the colors we choose,
Reflecting our journeys, the wins and the blues.
Life's effervescent, a bright symphony,
Evolving each second, from sea to the tree.

The Flourish of Flora

In gardens of whispers where the wildflowers
grow,
A tapestry blooms in the soft morning glow.
Petals unfurl in a glorious show,
Life's gentle heartbeat, a rhythm we sow.

From roots intertwined in the rich, fertile earth,
To blossoms that bring the world joyful mirth.
The flourish of flora, in colors so rare,
Speaks of resilience, nurtured with care.

Rebirth Under the Sun

Awakening softly, the earth takes a breath,
From ashes of winter, a dance with the death.
The sun stretches wide, painting skies in pure
gold,
Life's cycle continues, a story retold.

Petals emerge from their slumbering dreams,
Each morning a promise, a burst of new gleams.
Rebirth under sun, in the warmth we believe,
Every seed sown is a chance to achieve.

Joyful Burst of Colors

Splashes of crimson, a joyous parade,
Oranges and yellows, in sunlight they wade.
With blues of the ocean and greens of the trees,
A playful explosion that dances in the breeze.

In laughter of children, in art on the wall,
Each hue tells a story, a canvas to all.
Joyful burst of colors, in the heart they reside,
Uniting our spirits, like the ocean and tide.

Vibrant Hues of Tomorrow

In fields of gold where dreams take flight,
Brush strokes of dawn ignite the night,
Colors dance on a canvas wide,
Tomorrow's hopes, in hues, abide.

Crimson whispers in the gentle breeze,
Emerald laughter amid the trees,
Cobalt shadows in twilight's embrace,
A vibrant dawn, where futures trace.

Each petal unfurls with stories anew,
In vibrant dreams, we dare to pursue,
With every heartbeat, life's colors bloom,
In this vivid world, dispelling gloom.

Together we weave, through time and space,
In vibrant hues, we find our place,
A tapestry bright, our spirits entwine,
As vibrant tomorrows in sunlight shine.

Breath of the Earth

In the stillness, the whispers flow,
Nature's heartbeat, a gentle glow,
Mountains sigh as rivers weave,
In every corner, life takes leave.

The soil, rich with stories told,
Nurtures seeds of green and gold,
A symphony played by wind and rain,
The breath of Earth, a sweet refrain.

Ancient trees with arms outstretched,
Guard the secrets time has etched,
With every rustle, a tale to share,
Of love, of loss, of hope laid bare.

Through valleys deep and skies so wide,
The breath of Earth, our steady guide,
In harmony, we find our worth,
Connected by this sacred Earth.

Awakening in Pastels

Morning light spills through windowpanes,
Soft pastels wash away the stains,
Of night's shadows, fears that loom,
Awakening scents of springtime bloom.

Lilac dreams in the dawn's soft glow,
Peachy whispers of warmth bestow,
The world unfolds, so fresh, so bright,
Pastel hues in gentle flight.

Butterflies dance in a sunlit haze,
On petals painted in morning's gaze,
As nature sighs, a sweet embrace,
In pastel shades, we find our place.

So let us join this vibrant scene,
Awaken hearts and spirits keen,
In pastel palettes, hope will rise,
A canvas bright beneath wide skies.

Rebirth in Full Bloom

In every corner, life reclaims,
A dance of colors, wild and untamed,
From barren ground, to vibrant throng,
In full bloom, we sing our song.

Petals unveiled, like hidden thoughts,
In fragrant whispers, wisdom's sought,
The world awakens, the heart's delight,
In nature's arms, we bask in light.

Every sunrise, a promise made,
Of beauty born from shadows laid,
In gardens rich, new dreams are sown,
Rebirth finds roots where hope is grown.

Together we flourish, in radiant hues,
Rebirth in bloom, our vibrant muse,
With hands entwined, we tend our dreams,
In nature's splendor, love redeems.

The Symphony of Growth

In the hush of early morn, they rise,
Roots entwined, reaching for the skies,
Each leaf a note in nature's song,
Together in harmony, where they belong.

With whispers of wind, they dance and sway,
Learning the steps of the light's ballet,
In the garden's embrace, life finds its way,
A symphony echoing, come what may.

Seasons unfold like pages turned,
In the tapestry of time, each lesson learned,
From the smallest seed to the grandest tree,
Nature's orchestra plays, wild and free.

So cherish the growth, both fierce and meek,
For life's true beauty is found in the peak,
Of struggle and strength, of rise and fall,
In the symphony woven, we hear the call.

Dawn's First Petals

Awake, oh world, to the gentle light,
As dawn unfolds, banishing the night,
Petals unfurling, soft hues in the sky,
With whispers of hope, they reach up high.

The dew-kissed blooms greet the waking sun,
In a fragrant ballet, the day's begun,
Each blossom a promise, tender and bright,
Transforming the landscape with pure delight.

Through shimmers of gold, the colors blend,
A canvas of beauty, with no end,
They sway in the breeze, pure spirits free,
In the art of existence, they're poetry.

So breathe in the moment, cherish the see,
Of dawn's first petals, in harmony be,
For every day's gift in its simple way,
Reminds us to live, to love, to play.

Nature's Gentle Awakening

Beneath the frost, the earth's heart beats slow,
Though winter holds tight, there's warmth in the glow,
A whisper of spring in soft shadows found,
Nature awakens from slumber profound.

With each gentle rainfall, the whispers arise,
Tiny green sprouts reaching for azure skies,
In the stillness of dawn, the world holds its breath,
For life's tender touch is a dance with death.

Birdsongs weave through the veil of the morn,
Tales of resilience in beauty reborn,
A chorus of creatures, the world's sweet refrain,
In nature's embrace, we find joy and pain.

So pause for a moment, in quiet, reflect,
On cycles of life, and the love we connect,
For in nature's arms, we are all part of one,
In her gentle awakening, we see the sun.

Vibrant Life Anew

The canvas of life spills colors bright,
Emerging from shadows, into the light,
Each moment a brushstroke, bold and true,
In the gallery of existence, vibrant life anew.

With laughter like rivers, joy flows fast,
Searching for treasures, unearthing the past,
In every heartbeat, a rhythm unfolds,
Stories of courage, waiting to be told.

The petals of experience flutter and sway,
In the sunlight of hope, all fears decay,
With dreams like fireworks illuminating the night,

Together we rise, to take flight.

So embrace the colors, let spirits ignite,
For in this rich tapestry, we find our light,
In vibrant life anew, with each rising dawn,
We dance in the joy, until the day's gone.

Dancing in Dew

In the early morn, the grass does gleam,
Tiny jewels of dew, a shimmering dream.
With every step, the world does sway,
Nature's dance begins the day.

Beneath the sky, so vast and blue,
Whispers of wind bring life anew.
The petals flutter, the branches bend,
In this moment, time can't pretend.

As sunlight breaks, the shadows flee,
The day awakens, wild and free.
With every twirl, each drop does gleam,
We find our place in nature's dream.

So let the music of morning play,
As we dance in dew, and greet the day.
With hearts alive and spirits true,
Together we sway in the world anew.

Fragrant Expectations

In the garden where the lilies bloom,
Each petal whispers, dispelling gloom.
The scents of spring fill the air,
Inviting all to pause and stare.

Beneath the sun's warm, golden light,
The bees hum softly, a sweet delight.
With every breath, our hopes arise,
Fragrant expectations in the skies.

Time flows gently, like a stream,
Nurturing our hearts, igniting dreams.
In this haven, joy takes root,
Each fragrant flower, a pursuit.

So let us wander, hand in hand,
In a world where blossoms make their stand.
With every color, every scent,
Life's fragrant expectations are heaven-sent.

Sun-kissed Dreams

As the dawn awakes, the world aglow,
Sun-kissed dreams begin to grow.
Golden rays dance on the face of the earth,
A promise of beauty, a measure of worth.

In the fields where the wildflowers sway,
Nature whispers secrets, come what may.
Footsteps light on paths unseen,
Chasing the magic where we once dreamed.

Clouds drift lazily, a canvas above,
Painting our hopes with colors of love.
The sky is a palette, vast and bright,
Illuminating the day with pure delight.

With every sunset comes a new start,
Sun-kissed dreams live within the heart.
Embrace the moment, let life unfold,
In the warmth of the sun, our stories are told.

Blossoms of Tomorrow

In the quiet garden, seeds are sown,
Whispers of life in soft earth grown.
Each tiny sprout, a story to tell,
Of dreams and hopes where we now dwell.

With every gust of the springtime breeze,
Nature awakens, dancing with ease.
Blossoms of tomorrow in vibrant array,
A promise of color in shades of the day.

The sweetest blossoms, we tend with care,
Nurtured with love, forever rare.
And in their bloom, we find our grace,
In life's fleeting moments, we find our place.

So let us cherish, as life unfolds,
The blossoms of tomorrow, bright and bold.
Together we plant, together we grow,
In the garden of time, love's seeds we sow.

Joy in Adorned Branches

In the springtime's gentle embrace,
Branches dance with grace and cheer,
Bedecked in blooms, a vibrant lace,
Nature's joy, so pure and clear.

Whispers of life in every sway,
A tapestry of colors bright,
Each blossom tells a tale today,
Of hope reborn in morning light.

The air is sweet with fragrant tunes,
As petals pirouette on high,
Underneath the watchful moons,
They celebrate, they lift their sigh.

In this arboreal delight,
Hearts find solace, reaching wide,
For in the branches' joyous flight,
We find our dreams in nature's stride.

Sunlit Serenade

Beneath the sky, a canvas vast,
Where golden rays of sunlight play,
A serenade of summer's blast,
Awakens every heart to sway.

The flowers nod, their heads held high,
In harmony with breezes sweet,
With laughter dancing in the sky,
Each note a warm, enchanting beat.

Birds traverse the azure heights,
With melodies that weave and spin,
A symphony of pure delights,
As life anew begins to win.

So pause and listen, feel the glow,
In every song and every sigh,
For in the sunlit warmth we know,
Hope flutters gently, soaring high.

Buds of Hope

In the quiet of the morn's first light,
Tiny buds begin to bloom,
With whispers soft, they bring delight,
And chase away the winter's gloom.

Each tender leaf a promise made,
Of brighter days and skies so clear,
With every color, fear will fade,
As springtime sings, the heart will cheer.

Roots embrace the earth below,
Drawing strength from rich, dark ground,
In each small bud, a world will grow,
As life awakens all around.

So let us nurture hope's pure seed,
With patience and with gentle care,
For in each bud, a dream we heed,
A future bright, a love to share.

The Symphony of Bloom

In gardens lush, where colors blend,
A symphony of bloom unfolds,
Each petal sings, a joy to send,
In vibrant hues, their stories told.

The daisies clap, the roses sway,
With lilacs joining in the tune,
In rhythmic dances, night and day,
They paint the canvas, sun and moon.

From buds to blooms, the cycle spins,
With nature's clock, a steady beat,
A harmony where life begins,
With every fragrance, hearts repeat.

Embrace the music, let it play,
In every blossom, we will find,
The symphony of life today,
In nature's arms, our hearts entwined.

Tapestry of Colors

In the morning light, hues brightly unfold,
A canvas of petals, a story retold.
Crimson and azure, together they blend,
An artist at work, on whom we depend.

Gentle whispers of spring, in the breeze they play,

Painting the landscape, in vibrant array.
Each stroke a reminder, of beauty in flight,
Nature's own brush, crafting day from the night.

Through fields of daffodils, and forests of green,
A symphony of shades, so vivid, so keen.
The tapestry grows, as seasons entwine,
A world wrapped in colors, eternally divine.

So pause for a moment, let your spirit roam,
In this vast, colorful world, find your true home.
For every petal and leaf, every line and hue,
Is a chance to remember the beauty in you.

The Dance of New Life

From the earth's gentle breath, arises a song,
In rhythm with nature, where the heartbeats
belong.
Tiny buds break the silence, seeking the light,
Emerging from shadows, in vibrant delight.

In a cradle of soil, miracles bloom,
With each tender blossom, dispelling the gloom.
The dance of the sparrows, with joy so profound,
Signals the season where hope can be found.

As branches are swaying, under skies so wide,
Life swirls in the air, like a joyous tide.
New dreams take their flight, on the wings of the
morn,
Each moment a treasure, a promise reborn.

So let us rejoice, for the world is alive,
In the dance of new life, together we thrive.
With laughter and love, we share in the mirth,
Celebrating our bond, in the glory of earth.

Melodies of Nature's Renewal

The rustling leaves sing a melodic refrain,
Echoing softly like the gentle rain.
In whispers of wind, nature's chorus is found,
Harmonizing life in a symphonic sound.

The brook babbles sweetly, a tune from the past,
Flowing with stories of seasons amassed.
In every soft chirp, in the dawn's bright array,
The world comes alive, greeting the day.

As blossoms awaken, painting fields anew,
Each scent and each sound, like a dream coming true.
With petals and pollen, the air filled with cheer,
A symphony's birth, of warmth drawing near.

So listen intently to nature's own song,
In every heart's whisper, where we all belong.
For melodies linger, as sweet as can be,
In the rhythm of life, we find harmony.

Awakening the Garden

Under the veil of the soft morning dew,
Awakens the garden, with treasures anew.
A symphony stirs, as each flower unfolds,
Nature's embrace, like a story retold.

With hands in the soil, we tend to our dreams,
Nurturing seedlings, like flowing streams.
The promise of blooms, in whispers they speak,
In colors and fragrances, vibrant and sleek.

The sun kisses petals, as bees buzz with glee,
In this haven of silence, where we are set free.
Each leaf holds a secret, each vine a sweet tale,
In the heart of the garden, where hope will
prevail.

So cherish these moments, where life finds its
way,
In the dance of the bloom, in the light of the day.
For the garden awakens, with each breath we
take,
Unfolding our dreams, in the paths that we make.

9 789916 857748